Dedication

This book is dedicated to all the moms and those who take on this role, loving authentically on this journey, and especially to my mom Virginia Mae. There are no best made plans to being the best mom you need to be for you, your children, and your circumstances.

I love you Kennedy and Fanon. Be the best you…and to your children and their children.

Praise for Linda Cross and
The Pursuit of Momminess

"*The Pursuit of Momminess* is the ultimate culmination of Linda Cross's dedication to her kids. Linda documents her journey of raising two extraordinary children in today's media-saturated society. She reminds us why living in the moment is so important."

— Ingenue Faith Cobbinah, MD, Kansas City OB/GYN

"Linda Turner Cross has been an all-around supporter of her children, setting the standard for motherhood. She goes the distance to make sure they acquire skills above and beyond the average child so they will be prepared for the world. As a mother, Linda exposes them to things that help them grow academically, emotionally, and socially so they are well-rounded individuals, no matter the sacrifice involved. There is no doubt that *The Pursuit of Momminess* will help other mothers find a relevant perspective of motherhood."

— Rhonda Gray Reddick

"Linda Cross: Protective… Dynamic… Instrumental… Surprising… Sexy… Innovative… Rooted! All this in a package called, 'Linda.' She makes being 'The Working Mom' look so seamless that one would think it was effortless. She proves that, yes, ladies, you can have and do it all."

— Minister LaDonna J. Adams

"Being a mother is one of the greatest accomplishments Linda has achieved. Her motherhood journey is one of divine emotion that has created an incomparable feeling and an experience where she has not only nurtured her children but also herself. As her children grow and evolve, so does Linda in her pursuit of momminess."

— Lori A. Buckner

"I admire Linda for teaching and showing her kids how to live their lives to the fullest. She has ensured they understand the importance of self-worth, and she always makes time to bond and have fun with her family."

— Xoxo-Lasamy Sengsouriya

"I've always said this about my bonus daughter, Linda: In regards to her two children, my grandchildren (Kennedy and Fanon), she is their biggest motivator. I remember her talking about the plans she had for her firstborn before she was even conceived. Through Linda's gentle guidance, loving encouragement, and wise counsel, she has let them know they can do and be anything they want to do and be. I believe she has instilled in them the meaning of the quote, 'Nothing comes to a sleeper but a dream.' She led by example by showing them that faith without works is dead. She was their first and most important teacher. Her children are headed toward happy and successful lives, and I credit her momminess."

— Diane Turner, Linda's stepmother

"I am truly blessed and fortunate that God placed Linda in my life. None of my successes would have been possible without her support, determination, perseverance, and hard work. Linda's willingness to accept change and adapt to the needs of the family are impeccable. It is with great pleasure that I see her share her great gift with the world. Thank you, Linda, for being the best."

— Fanon Cross, Linda's husband

"In this little book, Linda Cross has delivered a plethora of wisdom. Beyond the expected stuff like changing diapers and discipline, she shares how you can encourage your children to grow into all they can be. Mothers will be surprised by the inspirational words here that will help them realize and embrace just how truly special their mommy role is."

— Tyler R. Tichelaar, PhD and award-winning author of *Narrow Lives* and *The Best Place*

The Pursuit of Momminess

How to Walk an Authentic Love Journey With Your Children

A Mom's Story

Linda Cross

AVIVA
PUBLISHING
New York

The Pursuit of Momminess: How to Walk an Authentic Love Journey
With Your Children

Published by:
Aviva Publishing
Lake Placid, NY
(518) 523-1320
www.AvivaPubs.com

Address all inquiries to:
Linda Cross
hello@pursuitofmomminess.org
www.pursuitofmomminess.org

ISBN: 978-0-578-39249-3

Library of Congress Control Number: 2022904772

Editing: Tyler Tichelaar and Larry Alexander, Superior Book Productions

Cover Design: Ieesha Chandler, Freelance Graphic & Web Designer

Interior Book Layout: Larry Alexander, Superior Book Productions

Every attempt has been made to properly source all quotes.

Printed in the United States of America

First Edition

2 4 6 8 10 12

Acknowledgments

With special thanks to my mother Virginia Mae Turner, an empowered woman who has taken my hand with faith, strength, courage, and belief.

Contents

Foreword

It is no surprise to me that my sister Linda has become an author. She has loved reading books since she learned to read. Every summer, we would go to the Hallmark store in downtown Kansas City, Missouri, to purchase the books we would read that summer. After leaving the Hallmark store, we would head to lunch, and the next stop would be the library in Lee's Summit, Missouri. Mama would say, "Select two books from the Hallmark store and two from the library." But at the library, Linda would check out a stack of books. With a big smile, she would say, "I have my books and I will read two a day."

Saturday morning, everyone would be in the car ready to go. Mama would ask, "Brenda, where is Linda?" I would reply, "Mama, she is looking for her book." Linda would arrive with one book in her purse and one in her hand. I never understood how Linda could read while riding in the backseat and not get car sick. As adults, when Linda and I began to have our own children, it was no surprise to my children when Linda purchased a book for them for every occasion. Linda is now a great-aunt and continues the legacy of buying books for birthdays and many holidays. Linda believes in education and the knowledge you can gain from reading books.

The Pursuit of Momminess will encourage you on your journey as a mother to inspire your child to pursue their greatest dreams. If you have already completed this journey, the book will give you the opportunity to reflect upon your fondest memories.

The truth is there are many ways to become the best mommy you can be. You will learn, whether you birth a child, adopt a child, or become a guardian, that your journey begins the moment you are face to face with your bundle of joy and it will last for the rest of their life. Allow Linda to motivate you to gain insight and inspiration and to reflect on your contribution to your child's dreams. Trust the journey of raising children who will spread their wings and sore like eagles.

Dr. Brenda Barrett, Mother, Life Coach, Leadership and Development Coach, and Best-Selling Author of *Set Yourself Free: Overcoming and Rebuilding Your Life!*

Introduction

"Grown don't mean nothing to a mother. A child is a child. They get bigger, older, but grown? What's that supposed to mean? In my heart it don't mean a thing."

— *Toni Morrison*

I t was early summer. It was the kind of day with extra-sunshiny rays to let you know summer is here. It was the kind of balmy hot that makes you only want to go outside after the sun begins to set.

That Sunday evening, I had been on a Zoom call with my church connect group. It was during the COVID-19 pandemic, so like so many others, we were meeting on Zoom to reduce the risk of spreading the virus. I remember my daughter Kennedy, a junior in college, faintly saying in the background, "I am going on a walk before it gets dark." She mentioned this knowing my call would go on for about an hour. We had started at 7 p.m. I then heard her say, "I want to go now so I can walk for an hour." Listening to both conversations, I nodded my head and continued on my call.

As my call ended, I got up and stretched my legs. Then I began moving around the house. The house was quiet. I realized it was now dark outside, and when I looked out the patio doors and above the palm trees, I could see the etching of the leaves swaying in the breeze. I could no longer see the shadow of the trees glistening in the pool water across the backyard. I turned, walked toward the hall, and headed toward Kennedy's room. I thought I would check in on her to see how her walk went. As I peeped in her door, there was no Kennedy. Her pink walls were silent. I looked up at her chandelier and gazed at the dangling crystal for a moment. I turned down the hall, where I could hear the sound of clicking and the soft, cheering sound of video games. When I checked in with my fourteen-year-old son Fanon, who was devoted to his games, he offered no details. I glanced at my phone. It was a little past 8:15 p.m., and darkness now completely filled the sky. I call Kennedy's name, heading back toward the front of the house. "Kennedy!" I called. Now I had the attention of my son, who came out of his room. I asked, "Is Kennedy here in the house?" Fanon walked back to her room and looked at me as if to say, "We both know she is not in there." But instead, he nonchalantly said, "No."

I decided to walk outside, but now another fifteen minutes had passed and it was after 8:30 p.m. I walked out barefoot, feeling the bumpy hot concrete on my toes. I walked into the street to see if I saw Kennedy coming. No sight of her. I no longer had my phone to check the time. I had left it next to the iPad from the Zoom call on the table. It felt like another twenty minutes had passed. Surely, she should at least be approaching our block. I decided to open the garage door and get into the car barefoot.

Where was Kennedy? I began to have a little rush of nervousness; after all, we had only been in Texas for about four months. We were still new to the area. Kennedy really didn't need to be walking at night in the dark, even if we had been here for a while. Houston was a big city, and we were still adjusting to the area. Now I was feeling a little perplexed. I was hot and flustered. I was not seeing Kennedy at all. I thought, *I don't have much time; every minute counts.*

I pulled out of the garage and drove down the street. Soon I was out of the neighborhood and on the main fairway. My pulse was increasing. Where was she? As I turned down the street, finally, I saw a white tennis skirt and our two little dogs, Lilo and Alex. Kennedy was walking on the sidewalk. I turned on my hazard lights in total relief. I took a deep breath and paused for a moment. I was just glad to see her and know she was home safe and sound.

Never mind that she was now twenty! I am still, like many moms, passionately in pursuit of momminess, doing my best to do what's right by my kiddos.

This book details my journey through life experiences that can help and remind you of the role we play as moms. I hope to inspire you, motivate you, or just make you laugh as you take this ride with me. My story offers vulnerable moments that let us know we are all human and have imperfections, but through perseverance, joy, laughter, tears, and plenty of valuable resources, we all have a passionate story inside of us about motherhood. My story just happens to be about the pursuit of momminess.

Chapter 1
The Pursuit of
Momminess

*"Mothers hold their children's hands for a while, but
their hearts forever."*

— Author Unknown

So, what does the pursuit of momminess really mean?

Let me start by saying, "I love being a mommy. I passionately love it and always will. I get butterflies just thinking about the years and special moments I have had with my kids. Was it wild and stressful at times, yes, but boy, every moment was worth it. Every moment was like a pursuit, especially when they were toddlers. Sometimes, it was a pursuit to keep up with them in the grocery store, or when we arrived at the restaurant and first sat at the table. The pursuit of who can grab the silverware first, then the drinks, then the meal, and so on! All those moments are mini-microcosms of your journey. They are what make us mothers smile and laugh or say, "Remember when?"

Think of what the pursuit of happiness means. It is defined as a fundamental right to freely pursue joy and live life in a way that makes you happy, as long as you don't do anything illegal. Isn't that what being a mommy is all about? Well, for the most part. It's about finding and sparking joy in your child's life. It's about all those moments of mini-pursuits. It's about living for those big brown eyes to light up when you walk into the room. Then, later in life, watching their eyes light up and their smiles spread across their faces when they are doing what they are inspired to do in life! It's about knowing that your pursuit of all things mommy had a little contribution to nurturing that joy. In a nutshell, that is it! That is the pursuit of momminess. That spark of joy and happiness that you were able to help instill in your child by actively participating in their life. To help connect the dots, to help inspire, to teach, to love, to find the resources, partnerships, discipline, coach, educate, appreciate, to nurse, to care—those are all the things that make up momminess.

When you first bring home your bundle of joy, you are excited and you have been preparing for this day. You have probably been reading about what to do next and what to expect, and even nesting in your home, getting ready for the big day, and the weeks, months, and years to follow.

You may have even consulted a few resources, maybe your parents or your mommy friends, and you have probably even received some unsolicited advice. We all can relate to that advice and the one friend who suddenly knows the ins and outs of nursing your baby; if you would let her, she is ready to pull your boob out and attach your child. But then you remember she has never nursed.

Being a good parent is knowing how to be vulnerable enough to pick up the phone and call your cousin whom you have not talked to in five years and say, "Hey, I am struggling here, and I heard you're a lactation coach—help me, please!" In those moments, we mommies let go of the fear of rejection, of not being the expert, and reach out, knowing the reward is greater than our sense of embarrassment. In those raw, organic moments, we find our real superpower is being free, being vulnerable, being open to becoming the best self we can be.

You are preparing to be the best mommy you can be. You are preparing for the journeys that are your child's life stages. Ready or not, once your bundle of joy comes, the journey begins. The beautiful thing about *the pursuit of momminess* is there are no steadfast rules to the journey. It's your beautiful journey of a shared bond between you and your child. This journey becomes rich from the experiences colorfully derived from what you make of them. While some might say there's only one true path to doing it right, the truth is there are many ways to be the best mommy you can be. What is even better is, for the most part, those big eyes are going to love you organically for who you are and not for any other reason. They are going to love you and your core, and that is just pretty darn special. They inherently know that you are human and flawed, and they love you for it all. Take a moment to breathe that in—they love you and who you are, for no other reason than that you are Mommy. That includes why they love you too, Dad.

Chapter 2
It's a Crazy Messy World but Someone's Got to Do It

*"I believe the choice to become a mother is
the choice to become one of the greatest spiritual
teachers there is."*

— Oprah

The pursuit of momminess probably doesn't sound like the realistic journey you were on or the one you are currently experiencing. You may not have even planned it. But no matter, even with careful planning, our kiddos kind of have a plan of their own from the moment of their arrival.

I never planned to be a mom. I remember planning to go to college and later thinking about getting married. I met my "person" as they say on *The Bachelorette*. We had fun and decided to get married. He asked, and I said yes, and at some point in our marriage, we became pregnant.

Did we talk about having a family? Yes. But we most definitely did not have parenthood scripted. In fact, I was a working mom, which is normal, but it makes planning parenthood a bit trickier. I was mostly just trying to figure this mom thing out as a balancing act, making sure it was tilted in the kiddos' favor.

It is important to note that we are all trying to figure this out. No mom is *the* expert—well, maybe the only expert is you, with your child figuring life out. Have confidence in your decisions, and believe in your parenting skills; that confidence makes all the difference in the world.

Give yourself grace when things don't turn out the way you envisioned. Take a moment or two to really let that set in. Give yourself grace. That is important to remember.

I will give credit where credit is due. I have an excellent partner who helped with everything. He changed a fair number of diapers and may have cooked the majority of the meals. It is important to let your partner be a partner.

But parenting is so much more than those experiences. Some days weigh heavier than others. But what happens for most of us is we end up loving the crazy days and spontaneous moments more than the others. After all, those days have more character. They remind us we are only human; we can only do so much.

How much we do when we are giving our best is enough. Know that there is no perfect way to be a mommy. When we release the idea of perfection in the moment and let life happen, we find joy. That is the S in the sweet spot. We let go of the notion that we are fully in charge, and we know that is okay. We realize we have to follow a set of rules, but we also rejoice in the moment—the "Hey, I got this moment" feeling.

Clarity Moment: If you are presently in the middle of the parenthood journey, know that you define what direction you're going, what works best for you, and the mommy journey you want to take. You've got this. Remember to give yourself some room for changes, flexibility, and grace along the way.

The reality is that it is definitely not all lighthearted and fun. As most moms will tell you, there is a ton of craziness and plenty of messes to go around. But if it were easy, it would not be a pursuit.

I am reminded of the movie, *The Pursuit of Happyness*. The father and son faced so many intense ups and downs and downs and downs. At some point, it was like "Can anything else go wrong on this journey?"

By the way, mommies, in the broadest sense, come in both genders and from all walks of life; aunties, uncles, and grandparents are included in this role. A mom's life is very similar to the ups and downs depicted in *The Pursuit of Happyness*. Being a mom is definitely not all roses and tulips.

Let me tell you a story. I will make it gender-neutral so no one can tell which kiddo it was. To save on embarrassment, I will not mention names. That day started out like any other Saturday morning. We were singing in the house, and the sun was shining through the windows. We were practicing and singing our ABCs. We were flowing in song; we were excited and having fun. I was so proud. Wow, my baby had it. We were pursing the alphabet, and to add another layer, the potty had just been mastered.

Going potty in the potty is a major deal—yes! It was an amazing, awesome Saturday morning. A new phase of life was beginning—going potty in the potty.

Then it was time for our famous bubble bath. Bubbles went everywhere. We were popping bubbles that looked like they could have been dancing in the northern lights. I drew the bubble bath. In went the toddler. Splash—we were all giggles.

That's when the Saturday moment changed.

I turned around, and in those bouncy bubbles, I saw little wooden logs floating. In hindsight, I realized maybe we got off the potty too soon. But in the moment, I thought, *Oh no!*

I lifted my toddler out of the tub and unstopped the water. I grabbed the phone while I had the toddler in hand, wrapped in a towel. I said, "Poop goes in the potty, not the tub" as I called my sister.

This may not sound major, but it was a major moment for me, and you really don't know when you may have a moment. Maybe I was too lost in the northern lights to come back to reality. I wanted this to be the perfect, easy, fun bath. I asked my sister what I should do.

(Was I kidding? I knew exactly what I needed to do—clean it up. But I panicked a bit.)

My sister said she was on her way. "Are you sure you are okay?" she asked. It was one of those crazy, messy moments, and I needed help. On that day, I reached out to my mom and my sister. Thank *God*, they both came over. They were both ready to help get the tub cleaned out and get me settled down. They decided to give me a break—my mom took my kiddo, and my sister took me for a ride.

The big lesson was realizing there will be days when you have to reach out. It doesn't matter what the situation, how big or small; in those crazy, messy, moments, you will need help. Although we may think we have it all under control, the reality is there is little we have under control. We are molding free spirits and free minds. We are like the guide on this journey, and it is okay to realize we may need to take a moment or reach out for help.

It's okay to know you need help. It's okay to know when you're raising these little humans, you have to lean in and expect the unexpected. Even when you think you've got it all planned, the plans change because you are not in the driver's seat. For me, this happened organically. I guess going poop is organic! I picked up the phone and started calling. I was blessed with two experienced moms who recognized my cry for help.

Sometimes, we don't make that call. But on this journey—the pursuit of momminess—it is vital to realize how important it is to ask for help when you need it. It is okay to be vulnerable, to let your children know you do not have it all figured out, and that sometimes, you need your village. It is okay to reach out with raw, authentic emotion.

I want to say it again: It is okay to reach out with raw, authentic emotion and seek help. We have all been there, and we will probably be back again, tomorrow, next week, next month—that is life, and it's okay and normal. Being vulnerable is our superpower. Seeking help is necessary.

Mommies wear so many different and unique hats. The hats can be protective, fun, colorful, big and floppy, small, or narrow and sophisticated, but one thing is certain: When we choose which hat to wear, generally, it is pretty organic and a spur-of-the-moment decision. We know when and where we need to put one on and when to take it off. At other times, however, we may struggle with when we need help taking them off—that is okay. Momminess is a journey, and we are all navigating the journey daily. We need to get to a place where we expect we will need each other and can drop our expectations of our kiddos and each other, thinking we are in control and have life all figured out.

We need to stop defining success by others' accomplishments. We need to stop showing up and asking someone what their kid is doing instead of asking how mom is doing. We also need to stop thinking we need to give advice as a comfort when someone is vulnerable; instead, we can just listen in those tender moments. Don't direct the person away from what they are organically trying to figure out. Just listen and comfort them, saying, "You got this, and how you choose to work this out will be okay."

As moms, our responses shouldn't be hollow accolades, but comments that reflect how the person seeking comfort truly is. You can't get help if you're not honest about where you are. And if you are uncomfortable sharing with your group, then maybe it is not your group. It's time to lean in with vulnerability—our kids need us to do this. The best we can do is be transparent and honest—then they will learn to trust and be vulnerable in their own lives.

Chapter 3
Am I Really Just
the Tour Guide?

"Children require guidance and sympathy far more than instruction."

— *Anne Sullivan*

What's this business about being a guide? As we go through these messy moments, and I mean figuratively and literally, we may hear "we are like a guide on this journey." We can direct our kiddo on their path, inspiring them with ideas and experiences, but it is, ultimately, their journey.

Despite being guides, we are also the baggage handler, ticket desk person, flight attendant, technician, and pilot. Let's be honest; we hold these roles sometimes willingly and sometimes whether we want to or not.

Reality check: We hold even more roles. It is like holding the baggage while trying to pull out our passport without dropping everything and we feel everyone is waiting. That's why knowing we are the guide is a lot to reckon with. We know our children will have to take the driver's seat, some sooner than others, but if we are not guiding them, then hang on tight everyone—it will be a wild ride.

Our children have to experience the journey wholeheartedly and learn to think for themselves. They have to do so, and they will attempt to do so, even with us holding on for dear life, if that is what it takes. It's a bumpy ride if you hang on too tightly. Quite honestly, we are not made to take on someone else's journey—and someone else includes our children. They have to learn to think for themselves organically, and when we think about it, they have been doing so since the moment they arrived.

I think back to something as simple as my breastfeeding, nursing experience. I finally got the feeding into a groove, and we were somewhat on a schedule. The flow was going great when someone decided to take charge of the nipple, and it was not me. It was mid-afternoon, and we were doing okay. Then all of sudden, I felt the gnaw of newly formed enamel ever so tightly go across my nipple. Yes, it was as painful as it sounds. That was definitely an organic moment, reminding me I was just the guide. Your kiddos will come up with ideas as they grow and develop. They really are in the driver's seat, and if you guide them, it can really be fun, interesting, and breathtaking.

Now, I am not saying we don't have opinions and "do what I say" moments because that is life and real talk. But when your kiddos start to know who they are, and who they want to become, all I can say is "Laissez-faire and let God. Ha!"

Understanding our children have freedom is so important because as much as we want to take ownership of all the good (and the bad) that they do, those are not our accomplishments. We need to accept the bad as well. We do not own our kiddos' choices. Does it hurt when they don't make the best choices? We better believe it stings, and we are prayer warriors before and after, but it never gives us the power to choose their path.

Wow, putting that into words brings tears to my eyes because as much as we may believe we are the best protector, prayer warrior, and all-around mom, we do not own our children's paths. They do. They own their path and their journey—they choose it. We are truly the guide. That is why we must be vulnerable, have faith, lean in, seek help, and find a proper village to surround ourselves with.

Chapter 4
Travel, Travel, and More Travel

"You're off to Great Places!
Today is your day!
Your mountain is waiting,
So... get on your way!"

— Dr. Seuss

Exposure, experience, and education—I think of them as the three Es. I didn't when we were traveling. We were just enjoying family time. I think this process just organically happens. Everyone is curious and naturally has questions, whether about where we're going or just from investigating the city, town, or location. Questions just begin to come up and evoke some conversation—sometimes quirky conversation and sometimes deep conversation. The difference can be as simple as driving past all the beaches in California, instead of driving through the hills of Arkansas.

As you can imagine, being a brown family riding through these different terrains, some interesting and important conversations come up. But remember, you're on vacation, and the goal is to relax and have fun.

We had our first child in California. Being in California made it kind of easy to get out and explore—we were in the land of all things exploration. We could not do enough, and still, to this day, I look back and think, *We didn't do enough in California.* Today, I don't have the little toddlers I once had, and we have had to make vacations pleasant during some very intense times. Like the time we drove their nana, who had once spearheaded our vacations, to visit her sister, who would be helping us because Nana had dementia. We drove to the tip of Mississippi but took time to explore Baton Rouge and New Orleans, Louisiana, to get an understanding of where Nana was from, while enjoying some of those famous sweet treats. Taking a moment away from the stress to realize that Nana was no longer the woman she once was and to celebrate that we still had her in our lives was a great choice. That may not sound like a dream vacation. But it was one of the most memorable times in our family's life together.

The family that plays together, stays together. Don't get me wrong. I am not saying we need to take the most extravagant trip in the world or the most adventurous. It doesn't have to be either. It just needs to be family time—with some snacks, overnight clothes if you are staying the night, and some good, old-fashioned fun.

Bring the phone for quick directions, photos, and maybe some movies if your trip includes a long drive or long flight.

Why is it so important to travel together? It gives everyone an opportunity to forget what is going on at school, in the neighborhood, and at work. It's a time to travel to another moment that frees your mind of all its baggage. This freedom shows you your today doesn't have to be your forever. Your today can be easily changed or removed, even if it is just momentarily.

You can take this experience back home with you, so when your child goes back to school, or just around the neighborhood, and those crazy issues pop up, they have perspective. They can say, "It doesn't have to be this way." You can back up those good feelings with moments from your vacation escape.

The world is full of places to explore together as a family. And maybe later, you can look back at those moments and find clarity. I'm not saying to run away from problems. But travel affords the opportunity to know there are other experiences to be had, and whatever issues come along the way, they do not have to be the *status quo*. It is a big world, and you do not have to be your environment. You can choose a different path. You have so many choices and opportunities besides what you may be doing now. Sometimes we all just need the hope and dream that we can do something different. Travel makes that dream tangible. We see we can do something different. We see the world we live in today is not one-size-fits-all. We see it's okay to fit into something different and live differently.

Chapter 5
Yes, It Is a Democracy, Even at Home

"The fastest way to break the cycle of perfectionism and become a fearless mother is to give up the idea of doing it perfectly—indeed to embrace uncertainty and imperfection."

— Arianna Huffington

Well, I am kidding myself if I don't own up to it. Yes, sometimes I have given as a reason, "Because I said so," or "Because I am the mama." And I may have used those reasons more than I would like to admit. I will say that giving such reasons doesn't have to be a bad thing some of the time. When we are in the trenches of all things mommy while raising our kiddos, sometimes a voice is needed at the table that says, "This is how it is going to be." When those moments happen, taking a stand is a good thing. It instills in you the confidence to speak, challenge, and set limitations for your children.

These skills will be important in your children's lives, so it is important for you to model these skills for them and let them also practice them. Even while living in a democracy, there has to be order. So what does your having confidence to speak up and set limits have to do with democracy for your kiddos? They will also someday have to express themselves and stand up for what they believe in. We have to give them that opportunity and allow them to practice this skill set at home where it can be done respectfully.

For example, take the lunchroom at school. We all know the kiddos who start the food fight. Not our kid, right? Haha! But do we know the kiddo who said, "I am not participating in that"? It is amazing when the teacher tells you your kiddo was the one who said, "We should not be doing this." Or, digging a little deeper, when your teenager is confident enough to say no to drugs and alcohol. This ability to stand up to peer pressure has to come from the experience of learning how to confidently express themselves. They need to know it is okay to speak up and say, "I don't agree. I challenge this." And that they can't do it just because "My mom said so." It has to be because they believe it is wrong.

That democracy household looks a little better now, I am thinking. Practice and good habits make facing those tough situations just a little bit easier. We all have had to role-play at some point; the purpose of role-playing is to give you that hands-on practice in action. Yes, it is tough sometimes to accept a difference of opinion in what you're doing, but it is vital to let our kids know they have a voice and they can make a decision. Still, it can be tough when you think your ideas are the best ideas, and then you hear that little voice saying, "Can we do something else?" or "That's not my favorite, or my first choice."

Part of that discomfort is knowing they will be making their own decisions one day. Now, I am not saying you have to go all the way to the left, but the confidence you build and instill in your child is worth going the other way sometimes. There will be plenty of moments when you get the opportunity to say, "I am in control," and "Because I said so." But celebrate those moments when they oppose you in a wise and thoughtful manner.

Chapter 6
It's Okay to Have Their Backs

"I will look after you, and I will look after anybody you say needs to be looked after, any way you say. I am here. I brought my whole self to you. I am your mother."

— Maya Angelou

I remember talking to a mom who said she just kind of went with the flow when teachers or camp people told her what was best. That is okay with some small stuff, but as moms, we need our own set of guidelines, and if the people we pay to interact with our children are not onboard, we have to have some serious discussions.

I had an experience where I didn't think a teacher was thinking beyond her own experience or providing a safe, supportive environment for my child. I tried to work with her and offer her a chance to see she was not meeting expectations, but she didn't hear me, so my husband and I worked with the system to remove our child from this person's classroom. We waited until the semester break and made the move without fanfare. It was quick and quiet, and our kiddo never knew why, but they were happy with the result.

It is important to act and make a change when you need to. Is it uncomfortable? Yes, but uncomfortable conversations are sometimes needed before we can progress.

We did three key things to make this the most supportive change for our kiddo:

1. We did not talk about the issues or solutions in front of our child.

2. We worked with the teacher outside of the classroom to identify the next steps.
3. We worked with the school's leadership to find the best outcome.

My child had no idea why that change took place. What they understood was they were experiencing something new, in a new classroom—one that fostered growth in a more productive environment.

It was also important that, as parents, we sometimes have to say "Not on my watch." We have to act. That is having our child's back. I took a stand. Together, my husband and I knew what journey we were on and the big picture of what that looked like for our child.

When you know the journey, and destiny, for your children, you will not risk accepting anything less. Sometimes the *status quo* does not work, so you have to be courageous enough to speak up. You can't get stuck in any system. You have to be progressive and foster change when the system is not working.

What about the mother I talked to whom I mentioned at the start of this chapter? I can't help but wonder if there was an underlying reason for her need to go with the flow. No way is perfect or right or wrong; you just have to take the path that is right for you in the pursuit of momminess with your children.

My takeaway was: You have a right to have your child's back. You have a right to support your child and take a stand when you need to. You can fall in line on other issues, but not when it comes to children.

Sometimes, we have to change the outcome, the trajectory of the story, when we want better outcomes. We do not have to accept the *status quo* if it is not for the best or for the benefit of our children.

The work you put in on the journey is so important. Remember, the investment you make now is key for tomorrow. Not all decision are easy, nor are they comfortable. Trust the process and the pursuit of all things momminess.

Chapter 7
They Are
Going to Fly

"My mother is my root, my foundation. She planted the seed that I base my life on, and that is the belief that the ability to achieve starts in your mind."

— Michael Jordan

Whether we are ready or not, our children are going to fly. We pray they are ready. As a mom, we pray, believe, and trust they will soar like eagles. Psalms 103:5 says, "Who satisfies you with good so that your youth is renewed like the eagle." Yes, like an eagle. The satisfaction comes from the journey when you are instilling your best thoughts and deeds into your child along the way. We are not perfect, but we can trust the work, words, and wisdom we instill.

Earlier, we talked about being the guide on the airplane. We wore a few other hats as well, but none of those hats were pilot hats. The kiddos are the pilots. From the moment they arrive on this earth, they are eager to take off. We equip them during our pursuit of momminess with tools to help them not only take off, but also to have a smooth landing. We have to accept that we can be the flight attendant, the baggage handler, and the ticket clerk, but we can never become the pilot. And sooner or later, our kiddos are going to fly.

Trust in all the things you have done along the journey and the things you could not do—trust in your faith.

"Mommy, I got this. You had my back, you held my hand, you hugged me tight, and you made everything all right. You stood up for me and even sat back down for me! You read me books, gave me journals, just for me to fill up. You made me lunch, made me laugh, made me smile. You even made me cry. You prayed for me, over me, and even prayed with me.

"But now it's a new day. It's a new day for you! It's a new day for me. For now I have my own back. I even sometimes hold your hand and make you smile. I hug you tight! I can make things all right when I stand tall or not at all. I read my books. I write in the journals day after day. I say a prayer for me, you, and the family.

"Mommy, I got this. Mommy, I got this journey. Mommy, I got this discovery. Mommy, I am blessed.

"Thank you, Mommy, for your pursuit of momminess."

We can trust the village we have leaned on, our exposure to resources, both intangible and tangible. Most importantly, we have to trust our kiddos to live the lives they choose.

A
Final Note

It is up to us to love our children. It is up to us to guide them. Our biggest task as parents is to love our children. We can love them into who they are meant to be.

Love is work, love is commitment, and love is time. Love is not focusing on your self-interest but humbly letting your child be who they are.

As we love without judging, we can provide input to guide them. In those non-judgmental moments, they come to know we have their best interest at heart—in our soul and mind. We cannot judge them into becoming who we want them to be. In fact, that can chase them away, if not physically, then mentally.

We are privileged to raise the future. We want our future to be better than our today. This can only happen if we love our kiddos for who they are. It is in *the pursuit of momminess* that we make this happen. The journey is better when it is organic and we pour love into the world of our children.

Ask yourself this question, "Do I truly want a carbon copy of myself?"

Doing the same thing over and over again and expecting a different result is often called the definition of insanity. Reproducing and copying the same behavior and expecting our children to follow will not make things better. It's like being our parents over and over again. At the least, we want a better version of ourselves and our journey.

I hope you will enjoy *The Pursuit of Momminess*.

About the Author

Linda Cross is the mother of two children: a daughter attending Florida State University in her senior year, and a son who is a sophomore in high school. Linda has been married for twenty-three years to her husband, Fanon Cross.

Linda was raised in Lee's Summit, Missouri. Her parents migrated there from Mississippi in the early 1970s.

After her parents divorced, Linda spent her teenage years being raised by her mom. She learned early about sacrifice, love, and empowerment. Linda's mom provided for her and made sure she was able to live her dream of being the first member of their immediate family to attend a university.

Linda attended the University of Kansas and graduated with a Bachelor's in Communications with a minor in East Asian Studies and African Studies.

The year she graduated, Linda met her spouse, and shortly after they were married, they relocated to California. There they began their family when their daughter Kennedy was born.

Shortly after Kennedy's birth, they returned to Kansas City where Linda was able to complete her Master's in Human Resources. As Linda learned to balance work and family life, her son Fanon was born in December of 2005. That same month, Linda completed graduate school.

For the last two decades, Linda has pursued her passion of supporting women. Linda founded *Needed Magazine,* a publication celebrating the stories of women in the community with the hope of inspiring women, moms, and girls.

Linda has partnered with non-profits and served on grant committees, lifting up grassroots organizations focused on empowering women and girls.

During the coronavirus pandemic, Linda was inspired to tell the story of her journey of love and passion for raising her children. In that moment, *The Pursuit of Momminess* was born.

Linda hopes to inspire moms all over the world through sharing her mommy love journey.

Find Out How Linda Can Help You

The pursuit of momminess is about being vulnerable. The pursuit of momminess is about being couragcous enough to feel pain. The pursuit of momminess is about being able to be real and authentic, and when lived out at its best, it is organic to the core. The pursuit of momminess is joy and happiness, with blinks of peace. It's heart-racing sunsets and easy morning sunrises.

Linda has opened up about her personal mom journey and has a simple message to share about this shared journey, *The Pursuit of Momminess.*

Linda wants to take you on her personal transparent journey of love. The very heartbeat of her being. A love walk of peaks and valleys.

Linda has a story to tell that exemplifies why it is important to live out your "mom" experience.

To follow your heart while guiding your child's heart.

To stand in your vulnerability. And at times, many times, to stand in the background to let the delicate wings of your little ones spread.

Linda motivates and inspires, and she will touch the hearts of others.

Linda's journey will offer support, build confidence, and allow other moms to know they've got this journey and it's unique to them.

Linda will share real-time parenting skills that will authentically fit in your life.

Find out how Linda can attend your next event or join your next podcast.

Contact Linda at hello@pursuitofmomminess.org.

www.ingramcontent.com/pod-product-compliance
Lightning Source LLC
Chambersburg PA
CBHW071357090426
42738CB00012B/3149